Truly You

Susan King

BookLeaf Publishing

Truly You © 2022 Susan King

All rights reserved.

No part of this publication may be reproduced, stored in a retrieval system, or transmitted, in any form or by any means, electronic, mechanical, photocopying, recording or otherwise, without the prior written permission of the presenters.

Susan King asserts the moral right to be identified as author of this work.

Presentation by *BookLeaf Publishing*

Web: www.bookleafpub.com

E-mail: info@bookleafpub.com

ISBN: 9789357613477

First edition 2022

Kelly

To stand strong along side someone you love as they break themselves open to heal past and present traumas, much like resetting a broken bone, is an admirable task.

Thank you for grounding me as I shattered and allowing me to glue my pieces back even in ways you didn't always recognize.

ACKNOWLEDGEMENT

To my Lifeboats during this time in my journey-
Kelly, Mom, Heather, Jamie, Shelley, Brittany, Angie and Ivy;
I said it in here but know that you make such a difference.

PREFACE

The last year has been the most transformative time of my life thus far. I am thankful for the events that have unfolded both well received and reluctantly endured and what those occurrences have required of me. As the layers of my carefully curated mask continue to fall away, I invite you along this portion of my journey in hopes that some long lost part of you might be discovered in the process.

She Is Mine

When you see me online- aglow and a shine
When you wonder: where was she when that girl was mine
When you long for the nights we spent wrapped up in love
And put me on pedestals, far and above

When you read of adventure, and journeys I'm on
And you wonder how we'd be, if we were not gone
When you think to yourself- now that's it, that's HER
And if she was here now we'd be better, you're sure

You should know that that girl you knew, didn't exist
And I'm not a version, of the one you once kissed
The pretense she was, was built special for you
And this person you see now, is all but brand new

I've untangled myself, from the pretzel I made
And scavenged to build, the foundation I laid

Standing here all aglow, a shimmer and shine
Is the me I was meant for, and she is all mine.

I Can't Go Yet

I can't go yet

Not while the stories pour through out me,
Twists and folds of plots reroute me.
Characters and foes are born
While words are crossed and pages torn.

I can't go yet

Not while views in far off lands unseen
Remain places I have never been
And soft and lavish grasses green
Remain untouched around the bend.

I can't go yet

Not while there are those I've yet to move
With kindest words and clever muse.
Illuminating glow I see
Deep within them shown to me.

I can't go yet

Not while my own stars are still so young
My brilliant words on shakey tongue.

So much to be so much to show
I cannot go is all I know.

Codependency

I see you spiral from afar,
I feel you lose your way.
Know what it's like to live through scars.
How do I make you stay?

Would it help for me to talk?
Translate your energy.
I can hold you as you balk.
The weight can fall to me.

Once again you're breaking down.
I'm here to pick you up.
Fixing you makes me feel found.
It proves that I'm enough.

Your shortcomings are what I crave.
To know that you can't leave.
You love to be the one I save.
Thus is the bond we weave.

Everyone Else Is Taken

I used to spend so much time,
Used to play the torture games.
Always asking myself why,
and feeding myself shame.

Twisting myself in
and stretching myself out.
Making myself fit,
for anybody who might doubt.

So they stay for just a while
and I get high on love.
My mask it fades off over time,
and they leave soon enough.

Once my choices were gone,
and I'm forced to just be
For a while I was alone,
Until I came to me.

It may have taken a little bit,
We might not have been sure.
But the pieces, all fit
and the paths unobscured.

In this mirror I stand,
I am whole finally.
The others be damned,
I'd rather be me.

The Little Things

It's the flavor of coffee in your cup just right,
The feeling of the workday end in sight,

It's the splendor of the evening light still left,
And the comfort of your home when it looks upkept.

It's the laugh of your lover when you make a bad joke,
And how they gazed in your eyes the whole time you spoke.

It's the one second extra of that goodbye hug,
And the warmth of a clean blanket all wrapped up.

It's the moments between from one goal to the next.
The things that don't require your very best.

It's the things that you turn to when you've nothing to give,
That make the life you've created one you can live.

Energy in Motion

Energy in motion
The pull of your heart
Energy in motion
It rips you apart

Energy in motion
Oh the things you can feel
Energy in motion
Every one of them real

Energy in motion
You can alter a room
Energy in motion
Make sure you're in tune

Energy in motion
Take control of your vibe
Energy in motion
Don't stifle your shine

Energy in motion
It's the key to it all
Harness your emotions
And you'll have it all

Sudden Onset

One day you wake up and all the sudden you're sick.
Can't get out of bed without feeling like shit.

Your breathing is short and your muscles all ache,
There's this pit in your stomach you can't seem to shake.

Everything you look up says you're dying somehow,
And everyone you talk to thinks you're just crazy now.

The doctors can't find a thing with you wrong
Some days even you think you're not being strong.

But you wake in the night pounding heart in your chest,
And a reel in your head of all the reasons to fret.

Is it the drinks that I had right before bed,
Or the caffeine I drank getting into my head?

You promise yourself you'll give it all up,
If it means that tomorrow you have better luck.

But by noontime next day alls well again,
And you ask yourself if you're now on the mend.

Was it imagined, a figment of your mind
Or is it a problem the doctors can't find?

Everything that once worried you into a fit,
Now the things you want back and the worries you miss.

Because now you see life as something deadly
Even after they tell you- it's anxiety.

Stand Out

Somewhere between childhood,
Jump rope and house,
When all was before her,
Her fire un-doused,

And the girl she is now,
Just outside office doors,
Dreading the wake up,
Each day a bit more,

She forgot all her dreams,
The impossible hopes,
Weren't impossible always,
Just fire to stoke,

But in all of the day to day,
Just getting by,
And societies rules,
About how she can't fly,

She got lonely somewhere,
And she tried to fit in,
But now she looks back,
Thinking what could have been.

Wonders

Badlands, Grand Canyon, Great Barrier Reef-
They all have in common this one awesome thing.

Neither one nor the other worked hard to become-
They allowed what was natural to build crumb by crumb.

So when the pieces aren't fitting together just right
Or the goals you keep chasing just won't take flight.

Remember what's meant to be isn't what's forced
But what occurs naturally creates what's adored.

Balancing Act

An hour in nature can create peace,
A run in the morning is good for release,

An evening of silence is a sought after break,
And a candle lit dinner can save some heartbreak.

But an hour in here and a moment in there,
Will only for now lift the burdens you bare,

The life you create must have balance to thrive,
Both self care and excitement so you feel alive.

Anxiety

When you're afraid of life
Because it might kill you
And you've lived through strife
But this kind feels brand new

You wanna drink it away
But that you fear too
Because one drink a day
Can send you well into

Fits of terror and sweats
So you abstain completely
But your fear you suppress
In hopes that its just fleeting

For a moment you think
The dread left you alone
And then in just a blink
The same panic is shown

What if my weak heart
Explodes in my sleep
Shatters me apart
Eyes open, I must keep

But what if the exhaust
It drives me insane
And I feel that the cost
Is far too much to take

Around every corner
There's a new thing to fear
Is disaster getting warmer
Or am I in the clear?

The Ones Who Are Missing

There they all are, so proud of you.
You're a star, you've hung the moon.
You've raise the bar, it's what you do.
It was so far, but look at you!

Your smile is there, they have earned it.
Though it's not fair, there is one wrong bit.
You want to share, you will admit.
But this despair, it doesn't fit.

The ones you want, they didn't show.
It shouldn't stun, you should have known.
Their lives they flaunt, your chapters closed.
You don't count, nor does your show.

So there you stand, with the ones left.
The ones who can, applaud your best.

Unfair to them, that you're so torn.
Grateful, yes, but still you mourn.

Two Journeys

Where before there were shadows, now I see light.
Where before We would argue, we no longer fight.

There was a time when we clashed, due to games we would play.
And whoever cared more, was the loser that day.

In every statement you made, I read a snide undertone.
In every smile you would wear, it was a sneer that was shown.

By the end we had twisted, and torn it apart.
Anytime we picked up, we'd be cut by the shards.

So we went our own ways, and took time to ourselves.
We each looked within, we found healing and help.

Now my demons and trauma, aren't poked by your words.

And we treat one another, with care and concern.

We'd both searched for a friend, who could match us truly,
Hurt by slights of the past, we couldn't care freely.

So thank you, my friend, for taking the time,
And being so open once I'd taken mine.

To come back around, and fine that in truth,
We were always well matched, as friends, me and you.

The Ones You Lose Along The Way

One day you look around
And it all seems brand new
As if your eyes were bound
Or obstructions in your view.

Colors are more bright
And situations clear
Things you thought were wrong
We're just things that you feared.

The pleasure that you feel
In shedding broken views
Almost enough to heal
The grief of those you lose.

Not everyone can come
They're not all ready for
The clarity of waking up
To things they have ignored.

To see you with this sight
Will highlight where they've failed
And in their own dark night
It's hard to watch you sail.

It hurts to see them lost
And you might try to help
But know that you must release them
If you want to save yourself.

Childless Exhaustion

When I fall down at the end of the day,
Say I can't go out there's just no way.

When I mention my aches and exhaustion inside,
I can't help but feel the judgmental eyes.

But you have no kids, society says,
You have so much time to decompress.

So I learn to keep quiet and leave it alone,
Decline plans without saying that I'm staying home.

Some days the existing is enough for me,
To ravage my peace, leave only debris.

Perhaps it's depression or just temperament,
But regardless of reason, there's no argument.

The fact is we all have a right to exist,
The right to retired when it hurts to persist.

Depletion of stores is not a rat race,
And killing yourself will not save you face.

Exhaustion is not a place to be best,
So care for yourself and don't judge the rest.

;

The trouble is not the spinning of thoughts,
The what ifs and if nots and everything lost.

The trouble is not the flat lined feelings,
Or the fact that nothing seems worth eating,

It's not that your limbs seem to drag through the day,
Or your eyes dropping shut while the tv plays,

It's the not knowing when you'll be back to yourself,
Like she's been put away up on a shelf.

She can see from a distance your life going by,
No telling when she'll be back from goodbye.

There's also the fear that one day she'll go,
And she'll never return leaving you stuck below.

Capitalism

Seems at the top you lose touch with life,
Think about profits instead of what's right.

The people below no longer connect,
Once a human before but now you forget.

No sitting or leaning for fear of the waste,
As if life quality is worth minimum wage.

If one person can rest for a second they're done,
Because why hire two when you could just pay one.

No thought of the moments when hours are paid,
So each second you spend will be one that they grade.

You spend four in the bathroom and two on your phone,
Doesn't matter if someone is half dead at home.

Because to them you're just bodies fulfilling a task,
And they'll stamp you defective if you drop the mask.

Put a smile on your face and be grateful for work.
And never forget that some have it worse.

But shield your eyes from the fact that the ones at the top
Keep stomping you down and don't plan to stop.

To my Lifeboats

Thank you to those who have heard it all twice,
Who've listened and nodded and smiled real nice.

I know it's sometimes redundant and long,
And sometimes resembles a replaying song,

And I swear every time I press play once more,
There were several times I pressed mute before.

But the song in my head has no such button,
So the song plays and plays until sleep can be summoned.

But it helps to have sounding boards with a response,
To catch and reroute me when I am lost.

Your ears are a treasure, your words a life boat,
When I'm treading water you keep me afloat.

So whenever you think it all seems the same,
Know what a difference your presence has made.

For lack of a mute inside my brain,
You've saved me from 'off' on this dwindling flame.

My Reasons

The things that keep us here aren't things,
They're angel heartbeats with no wings.

The ones we put our hope into,
And ones that always see us through.

The woman who sees everything,
And puts up with the annoying,
And sometimes does the cutest stretch,
And never leaves without a peck.

The little girl who had it hard,
But never lets them take the part,
That makes her shine bright like a star,
And will for sure take her so far.

The vibrant boy dancing off beat,
To every song with happy feet,
Who cuddles even in his teens,
A love that couldn't be foreseen.

It isn't things that keep us here,
It's those we love and hold so dear,
That keep us going when it's hard,
Cause leaving them would break our hearts.